Toddler Parenting

How To Communicate and
Use Effective Discipline
To Raise a Happy and
Self Confident Toddler
Without The Tantrums!
(Best For Ages 1-4)

Laura Stewart

First Printing, 2013

ISBN-13: 978-1492367574
ISBN-10: 1492367575

Printed in the United States of America

Table of Contents

INTRODUCTION

Parenting is probably one of life's most rewarding experiences and one of the most important jobs in the world. But once your baby starts walking, life can turn upside down, because you no longer have the same control. How fantastic it would be if toddlers came with operating instructions!

If only I had had access to this information when I was a young mother with twins and had three toddlers on the go. As a teacher still dealing with young children and the grandmother of toddlers, I have a wealth of research and experience. Here are six concise and simple chapters full of valuable information.

You will learn:

- how to create a happy, calm and loving environment for your family

- how to help your toddler master the important skills of walking, talking, eating, dressing and socializing

- about habits that help build a strong and trusting relationship with your toddler

- effective communication skills to practice with your toddler

- strategies to use when your toddler misbehaves - including dealing with temper tantrums

- how to use loving discipline to create a win-win for you and your toddler

Wouldn't it be great if it was all peace and harmony while they are so cute and fun to be around! As parents we want to feel that we're producing well behaved and happy children - as long as they abide by our rules.

We like to think that we have enough common sense to raise our kids sensibly. But for most of us, dealing with a toddler needs more than a touch of common sense.

Of course we want to know that we're doing the "right" thing - particularly if it's our first child. However, during the toddler phase the learning curve for both parents and toddlers is so steep that many parents find life quite nerve racking. It's hard to keep up as our toddler leaps out of control from one major milestone to the next.

To be unbiased in relation to gender, I refer to boys in the odd chapters and girls in the even chapters.

1 SETTING THE SCENE

Believe in your ability

It's not always as easy as it sounds, but the old adage "fake it till you make it" certainly holds true when parenting a toddler. It's OK to pretend, even if you don't feel it. You'll naturally become more confident with practice and experience.

You'll also discover that you're not alone as you tilt and swerve on this rollercoaster ride. If you believe that you can do it, your sense of confidence will give your toddler the vitally important reassurance he needs. For some, the ride is bumpier than others because all toddlers are different, so don't compare and don't despair.

Do you have support?

You are fortunate if you have a support network. Child rearing isn't easy on your own. Hopefully your relationship with your partner is strong and you have each other. If not, make a point of turning to family, friends or a support group. Reach out for the support you need so you can focus on being the best parent that you can.

Toddlers pick up vibes

One of the important things to understand is that you and your partner are your toddler's role models. If you want your toddler to be happy, loving and respectful, you need to be happy, loving and respectful with each other and with other family members. When you are tense your toddler can pick up your vibes. Don't be surprised if he reflects back that tension in some form of misbehavior.

Agree on the guidelines

It would be really fantastic if carers agree on the rules and guidelines around routines and expectations in your household. If you are both clear about what is acceptable behavior, your toddler will know where he stands.

In an ideal world both parents would agree, but often reality is a different story. Take heart if you can relate to this. One consistent carer can make a difference and still build the relationship you want with your child.

It would be especially helpful if you could let members of your extended family understand your wishes about parenting. If they are willing to use the communication skills you'll learn in chapter four, you have an added bonus!

Set the example

Toddlers' brains are like sieves during this phase of their lives and they will learn by imitation. They will copy your values and attitudes as well as your behavior.

If you practice self-discipline, your toddler is much more likely to follow your example. If, on the other hand you smack or yell at him, don't be surprised if he hurts or yells at others. It might be hard to continually keep your cool, but toddlers become easily confused when they get mixed messages.

Have realistic expectations

The more that you understand and accept your toddler's limitations, the easier your life will be. The following list is not exhaustive and certainly not meant to be critical, but it may help you set realistic expectations of your toddler's behavior. It is not gospel, because every toddler is different. But take heart if your toddler shows signs of being like this; he's normal.

• Toddlers lack reasoning skills. Their brains are not developed enough to understand as much as you probably think they do.

• At twelve months, toddlers have no sense of time. They live for the here and now.

• Toddlers show little self-control yet they can exert an enormous amount of power over those around them.

• Toddlers are self-centered and hate being ignored.

• Toddlers are messy and usually untidy until they are at least three.

• Young toddlers have little idea about being gentle, careful or polite.

• Toddlers ask questions endlessly.

• Toddlers can get excited really easily and a noisy environment can make it worse.

• It is easier to "toddler proof" your home than to have unrealistic expectations about respect for property.

• Toddlers are super sensitive and can pick up on tension in their surroundings.

• All toddlers are different. Life will be a lot easier if you accept your child's temperament and inborn personality.

Children want structure

Just as we function more effectively when we have structure in our day, your child will be more settled and confident if you follow a regular daily routine. Predictable routines reduce stress and give toddlers a sense of security in an otherwise overwhelming world.

A regular routine also helps toddlers gain a sense of time. They will first understand about meal times and then bed time, bath time and snack time. Initially fix your routine around these activities.

It is a good idea to set routine times for activities such as playing with toys, playing outside or playing with you. A regular story-time routine is really important. For activities such as watching TV or playing on the iPad, set certain times with a pre-defined time limit.

Set limits

Toddlers need to know what is acceptable and what isn't. Sometimes they go at breakneck speed to see how far they can push and test every boundary possible. They don't know when to stop.

So that they feel safe, secure and in control, toddlers need to know what is OK and what is not. Rules around hitting, meal times and no-go zones such fireplaces and breakables are a good place to start. Make sure that you and your partner agree on the "house rules" so that your toddler cannot play one off against the other.

Be consistent

Once you set guidelines, it's important to remember them! If we say "only 30 minutes on the iPad a day" we need have a mechanism in place so that we can stick to the rule. It's easy for toddlers to get confused if the rules keep changing. Consistent guidelines, routines and limits will make life a lot easier.

2   IT'S A CRITICAL PHASE

Did you know that toddlers learn more between 12 months and three years old than during any other stage throughout their whole life?

Many carers don't realize the huge impact that their parenting has on the future life of their toddlers. During this crucial phase of physical, mental and emotional development, toddlers need a solid sense of belonging and importance in a safe and happy environment. Secure toddlers are much more likely to grow into stable and mature teenagers.

Toddlers don't only learn to walk, talk, feed, dress and socialize. They also learn right from wrong, they learn to control their impulses and learn to solve problems. As they strive toward a sense of self and autonomy, it is actually quite a frustrating time for little people, so they need more of your attention and reassurance now than they ever will again.

Walking

How exciting it is to see those first few steps! As your toddler gains confidence, she can also become frustrated because she falls over often. Similarly parents' pride often turns to fear about them hurting themselves. You'll do your toddler a great favor by allowing her to fall and learn to get up all by herself. This will build her confidence and a sense of capability.

Children by nature are trustworthy. Although it is very important to teach caution around danger such as roads and driveways, over protection in other aspects of life can result in your child losing her sense of adventure.

By allowing your toddler to take risks, you are showing her that you trust her. You only need to be at arm's length in case of a dangerous fall. For example, let her climb up the stairs without your help. Just keep behind her.

Talking

Toddlers will continue to babble for some time, but as they learn words they are bound to make mistakes. They want to feel understood when they speak, so take care with your response. Repeat her phrase back to her using the correct words and pronunciation. For example reply to: "Dat tat" with "Yes, that's a cat". You will build her confidence and ability by speaking slowly and clearly using simple words and short sentences.

Read to your toddler regularly, pointing to objects that she can repeat back to you. Singing nursery rhymes is another great way to help your child develop her verbal skills. Toddlers love rhyme and repetitive phrases that they can mimic.

As they are practicing their newly found skills, toddlers will repeat the same questions over and over. Your patience and attention will pay off in the long run.

Eating

A regular routine is your friend. Make food more appealing to your toddler by feeding her small servings. As she learns to feed herself, don't make it hard on yourself. There's no need to offer choices all the time, but if you do, try just two healthy ones. For example: sultanas, cheese – or nothing. Children won't starve from stubbornness.

For older toddlers, another strategy is to have them choose just two foods that they don't want to eat. They can change their mind after a week or three, but in the meantime it gives you a lot of leeway with many other food choices.

It will be easier to go shopping after a mealtime than before. If you can, avoid the candy aisle in the supermarket.

It is good practice to eat with your children as soon as is practicable. This shows them respect and is the easiest way to teach table manners. Since toddlers are uncoordinated and messy, it's good to help them learn just one skill at a time.

Dressing and undressing

This can be a really exasperating time for busy parents because it takes time for children to learn to coordinate their brains, arms and fingers. You need to allow time and give them some choice.

Choice gives toddlers a sense of accomplishment and self-sufficiency. Just like food, you could offer just two choices. Ignore refusals. Continually repeat the same offer calmly with a firm voice.

Toddlers love to feel adequate and helpful, so this is a good opportunity to ask them to help you by dressing themselves. Remember to show genuine appreciation for their help: "That was great dressing, Sweetheart! Now Mommy is ready too!"

Particularly for girls, one time saving routine (with your toddler's help) is to lay out tomorrow's clothing the evening before.

Socializing and play

From twelve months toddlers learn the crucial skills of interaction and integration that will imprint on their behavior for the rest of their life. They learn to share, to compromise and to consider others.

Until about two, toddlers tend to play alone, but alongside each other. While they are doing this, they observe other children at play. This is how they gain confidence in their own abilities and learn about sharing and taking turns.

Because all toddlers are different, they will have different preferences for the type of play that they engage in. Various types of play will facilitate your toddler's mental, emotional and social skills in different ways.

1. Physical play helps toddlers gain physical coordination. In turn, running, jumping and balancing helps children gain confidence. They also gradually learn to consider others by taking turns and sharing.

2. Imaginative play is a great way to help your child express her thoughts and emotions. This is why children love their teddies, their dolls and their superhero figurines. Toys that reflect the real world such as farm animals, train tracks and dress ups all help to develop their imagination.

3. Reading to your toddler helps develop her concentration and vocabulary skills as well as her imagination and awareness of the world around her. It is good to choose simple short books where you can point out objects that your little one will recognize and be able to repeat back to you.

4. Creative Play using crayons, play-dough, colored paper, glue, paint and paint brushes etc. helps develop hand-eye coordination and concentration. Toddlers love to have you involved so this is also a great bonding activity.

5. Problem Solving play such as jigsaws, Lego and matching games help toddlers develop concentration and problem solving skills. If they get overwhelmed by having too many choices, be clever about removing some of the pieces so that they have less options to choose from.

Television and Tablets

TV has long been a favorite baby sitter for busy parents. However too much time spent on TV and electronic games can result in children becoming easily bored because they rely on them for constant entertainment. Ideally you should structure set times for these activities.

It is a good idea to watch selected programs together with your children – for example, a little while before story time at night.

3 BUILDING A RESPECTFUL RELATIONSHIP

Because toddlers have limited reasoning skills at twelve months, you are their main teacher. It is so easy to get caught up in the everyday routines and hiccups, that it can be easy to forget your role.

Here are some important habits that will help develop trust, respect and cooperation between you and your toddler.

1. Attention

Children want to feel that they matter. They only way a child learns that he is important is by receiving attention. You may well have trouble spreading your time, but it is crucial to give your child as much quality attention as possible.

It is difficult (and unhealthy) to give toddlers such devoted attention that they are continually dependent on you for company. Although every child needs to know that he is loved, it's also good to encourage your toddler to amuse himself.

Toddlers may still suffer separation anxiety so they need your undivided attention regularly to continue to feel secure. Tell him you love him morning and night. Hug him lots and touch him often. Often just being near to your little one while he is playing is all that is needed.

Attention is particularly important when welcoming a new sibling into the family. Oftentimes it helps if you put your toddler first. Even if your new baby is crying for a feed, take an extra couple of minutes to ensure your toddler is settled with an activity or a snack. This way, he is less likely to act out while you are attending to the baby.

2. Special time

Have a special 'Me Time' routine; one-on-one quality time at a similar time every day. If you make it before bed, you can talk about all the good things that your toddler did and enjoyed in the day and what tomorrow will bring.

If you have more than one toddler this is a good way to help the older one to learn about sharing. He can see that his little sister has her special 'Me Time' too. Watching siblings have 'Me Time' will also help your toddler learn patience.

3. Accentuate the positive

Always accentuate positive behavior. This helps build self esteem and a sense of prowess. It's too easy to get exasperated by the irritating things that all toddlers do and just let the good behavior slip by unacknowledged. By acknowledging even the littlest of good behavior, whether it be sitting still for a bit or keeping quiet when you have appreciated it, you teach your toddler which behaviors you like.

Children are not naughty, but they can do naughty things.

Distinguish between your child and his behavior. Always acknowledge behavior that you want to reinforce - not the child for doing what he did. For example, rather than saying "What a good boy for dressing yourself!", say "Hey that's good dressing!"

There is a difference between unconditionally loving your toddler versus acknowledging him for the good things he does. If you only link his goodness with good behavior, this can lead him to believe that he's only OK when he does the right thing. Children need to know they are OK in themselves, whatever their behavior.

4. Affection

Demonstrate lots of affection. This doesn't always come naturally, but all children need genuine affection.

Here are a few ideas:

• Practice using a loving and proud tone of voice when giving praise. "I love you sooo much!" "You're just so special!"

• Show him you're happy to see him in the morning.

• Make a point of making eye contact often.

• Give your encouraging remarks some loving oomph.

• Remember to give him lots of hugs, kisses, smiles, winks and high fives.

• Use affectionate names such as "Sweetheart" or an endearing nickname..

• Tell him you're happy he's yours.

• Look him in the eye as you tell him you love him at least twice a day.

5. Children like to feel useful

Make yourself team-mates where you are the leader and he is your important helper. Rather than instructing your toddler to do things, asking him to do something "for you" is a great way to foster cooperation: "Honey, can you find your shoes for me?"

He could also help you with household chores such as taking something to the laundry or picking things up off the floor as you vacuum. Of course then acknowledge his help by thanking him. A simple sentence such as: "Thanks Sweetie, that was a great help!" will build him up so much more than if had you just told him to do something.

6. Choices and opinions

Look for situations where you can give him choices and ask for his opinion. This will help him learn to make decisions. Keep the options limited to two. For example what fruit to buy - "Will I buy apples or bananas?" or what veggies to cook for dinner - "What will I cook - peas or broccoli?"

7. Get physical

Get down to the floor often. This is the best place to build a strong, secure relationship because you are at your toddler's level. This is also a good place to practice discipline (covered later). The floor is a great leveler. Lie down and play. Have your toddler crawl over you, tickle, wrestle and giggle. Be the underdog. Be the clumsy one. Pretend to be blind, confused and forgetful. Don't make it too long though. Watch for signs that your child is getting over-excited or a squabble between siblings is looming.

8. Random acts of kindness

Giving your toddler unannounced gifts that are not linked to any specific behavior helps boost his self esteem and sense of importance. It doesn't mean toys. It might be a big box or an old blanket, some flowers or a cool pair of socks. You may make a special treat of their very favorite food once a week. Acts such as this will teach them about kindness.

9. Acknowledging feelings

Growing through the toddler learning curve is not easy for them. As children learn to solve problems, they need your support and encouragement. Don't ridicule or punish a toddler if he makes a mistake - even if you don't like the consequences.

Toddlers need understanding and unconditional love during these years more than at any other time. Toddlers whose feelings are lovingly acknowledged are much more likely to grow into emotionally mature children.

10. Praise

Let your toddler overhear you acknowledging his good behavior to another person. For instance, you could make this a regular routine when Dad comes home. It may be Grandma on the phone.

4 COMMUNICATION

It's Not What You Say, It's How You Say It

It is a well established fact that verbal dialogue is only a fraction of the actual communication that occurs between two people. This of course applies even more with toddler communication because they simply don't have the verbal skills yet. Let your toddler know that you respect her and she is important with your actions, your expressions, your tone of voice and importantly, your listening skills.

Gaining attention

A really effective way to gain your toddler's attention is to use two sensory mediums at the same time. Your toddler is bound to take notice if you touch her and look her in the eye as you say her name.

Listen with respect

When your toddler babbles on and on to you, do your best to listen with respect. You may struggle to understand what she is saying, but even a short response such as "uh-huh" indicates that you heard and that you value her as a person.

Parents who don't REALLY listen to their children are sending a clear message that they are not important and are unwittingly planting the seeds of low self-esteem. Toddlers crave positive attention and if you don't respond, they may simply use another method to get your attention – quite likely an annoying one.

Active listening

In "The Happiest Toddler On The Block", Harvey Karp, MD uses the term "Fast-Food Rule" to describe the most effective way to communicate with toddlers if they are upset. A good restaurant waiter always repeats your order back to you before heading to the kitchen.

This concept of communication originated back in the 1950's by a famous psychologist, Carl Rogers. Rogers used the term 'Active Listening' to describe a way of communicating where the listener actually reflects back to the speaker what he thought he heard him say, in his own words.

Active listening is such a powerful way for you to connect with your toddler! It will work wonders, both in calm and difficult times. Toddlers are constantly practicing their speech, and if we repeat back to them what we thought they said, it will make them feel important and valued.

Firstly it's a great learning tool. Active listening will help your little one as she is practicing her speech if you clearly repeat her words back to her. For example if she says, "Can I have this? I really love this doll!" you could reflect back with "You love this doll, you really love it, don't you!" Just because you are reflecting her feelings doesn't mean that you're agreeing to buy the doll.

Secondly, active listening is a great way to stop an upset escalating into an uproar. When toddlers are screeching or whingeing, of course we want them to stop. You may be annoyed or exasperated, but an agitated reaction makes a toddler feel discounted or unimportant.

If you reflect back to them what you think they are upset about they're more likely to feel understood. Once they notice that you are listening, they're more likely to settle down quicker. They want you to understand about their frustration or anger without getting into trouble.

Once they have calmed down, you can then divert your upset toddler's attention to something else.

Active listening by reflecting feelings to your toddler may feel a bit silly at first, but once you practice it and see how clever it is, you will find that it works in all sorts of situations – not just with your child.

Here are a few important guidelines to follow:

1. Practice empathy

Active listening is by definition empathic. The idea is to genuinely care and show the other person that you really understand how they feel. It doesn't mean that you have to agree with them. You can care without agreeing. For instance, responses such as "uh-huh" "wow!" or "Oh no! You must feel sad" generally work with people of all ages, not just toddlers.

2. Mirror some emotion

As you repeat back what your toddler said to you in your own words, also mirror some of her emotion. For example, you might respond to an upset "That's MY teddy!" with something like "It's not fair! That's your teddy!" with some emotion in your voice and facial expressions to emphasize that you understand her feelings when her brother steals her teddy.

3. Take turns to talk

Once your toddler has let off steam, THEN respond. Don't block her by interrupting. Use some "uh-huhs" until she has had her say. Then it's your turn. Respond with respect. An annoyed reaction will not help. It is so easy to make our children wrong with reactions like "Just stop it! You're making me angry!" Instead, keep reflecting back what your toddler is saying (in your own words) until she settles.

Once you've done that, THEN you may distract her, help her solve her problem or offer her options. If your response is reassuring she is more likely to trust you, but you can still be firm at the same time. Just do your best to remain consistent.

If you try to distract your child without giving her the respect of listening to her feelings first, it can be quite hurtful. Your toddler may comply by pushing her feelings down, or she may just scream even louder to get you to listen.

Parents often try to diffuse upsets by telling their toddler that everything is OK. However if you are actually trying to stop her from becoming upset, you're telling her that it's not OK to have feelings. Toddlers need to feel safe and know that it's OK to have upset feelings.

But it's not OK for children to have to put on a happy face as they cover hurt feelings inside. Quashed feelings could well come to the surface eventually and manifest as rebellious or other dysfunctional behavior in the future.

4. Use "When You – I Feel" messages

Once your toddler has calmed down you have the opportunity to tell her how you feel. If you have listened and really care about her upset feelings, it is more likely that she will listen to yours.

This is a great skill to learn because you can use it with anyone that you have an emotionally close relationship with. Here is a simplified version of what you could say: "When you do X, I feel Y". So with your toddler, you might say, "When you keep whingeing, I feel sad. Can you ask nicely instead?"

By telling your toddler that you FEEL something you're helping her become aware that other people have feelings too. By asking her clearly for what you want, she isn't left wondering.

5. An upset toddler doesn't listen

If we are angry, it's much harder to listen objectively. This applies to your toddler as well. There is no point in trying to reason with a screaming child. Even offering alternatives is likely to fail. You may get your way eventually, but if your toddler doesn't feel understood, the experience will be stashed away in her sub conscious.

If you discount or ignore your children's strong feelings often enough, you are likely to be dealing with problem behaviors throughout their childhood.

6. Behaviors to avoid

For as long as we know, parents have tried all sorts of tactics to stop a toddlers' whingeing or emotional outbursts. The trouble is that:

- Shouting will teach your toddler that it's OK to shout at others.

- Ignoring will tell your toddler that she doesn't matter – that she's not important.

- Trying to reason with an upset toddler wastes energy.

• Empty threats teach your toddler that you don't mean what you say.

• Putting children down will teach them that they are no good.

• Verbal attacks such as name calling and hurtful labels like "bad" or "dumb" can affect a child's self esteem so much that it can last a lifetime.

• Exaggerations such as "you never …" or "you always…" are not only untrue but are completely counter-productive, harmful and are likely to put your toddler on the defensive.

5 DISCIPLINE

Discipline is not about punishment! We all feel more secure when we know exactly where we stand. Discipline is about teaching and guiding your toddler so that he learns right from wrong and learns about taking responsibility for his actions.

When you discipline your toddler with love you help build his self esteem. When you reward and encourage the behavior you want and provide alternatives to unwanted behavior, toddlers learn how to get what they want in a positive way. This is the key to raising independent and cooperative children.

Every family situation is different, so nothing written here is set in stone. You may have been blessed with an angel of an infant but your toddler could just as easily have the temperament of a terrorist. Discipline will definitely be more challenging for some parents than others.

It's important to not blame yourself if your infant was born with a fiery or determined personality. If you fall into the trap of comparing your toddler's temperament with others, you are adding to the already challenging job you have on your hands.

Three factors for effective discipline

1. Communication

We talked about effective communication skills to use when your toddler is either happy or upset. But when he is misbehaving, here is another technique. Squat down to his level and give him a clear message. Speak respectfully. Use simple words and with a firm tone of voice, look him directly in the eye: "George, please don't hit. Hitting hurts people!" Your toddler can't ignore you if you touch him and look him in the eye as you use his name.

2. Consistency and Structure

This is also worth mentioning again. A happy household will have only one set of rules and a regular routine. If a toddler can get away with murder one day but is then reprimanded for a minor misdemeanor the next, he is likely to be confused or frustrated.

Toddlers don't handle confusion well at all. They are more likely to act out and see how far they can push the boundaries. Remember, they are aiming for autocracy and independence.

3. Be Positive

In the first chapter I mentioned it was important to exude confidence because it shows your toddler who is in control. Children WANT TO respect, so show them you are worthy of it by having a confident and positive attitude.

Making rules – setting boundaries

Every one of us needs discipline, whether a child, teen or adult. We only have to look at the regions of the world where conflict is rife to see the effect of rules that are either too strict, inconsistent or non-existent.

Just as we live in a society with clear guidelines for right and wrong, your role is to teach your toddler right from wrong in a clear, kind and respectful way. The values they learn at home will affect the way they socialize in the world.

Your discipline will be more successful if you have set some guidelines and consequences before situations arise.

Pre-determined consequences will prevent you from dishing out impulsive and unrealistic ones. Of course you don't have a crystal ball, but here is a small sample of basic common-sense rules that you can add to. You could post your rules up somewhere to serve as a reminder for yourselves.

- Be kind to each other

- Keep your hands to yourself

- Use an indoor voice in the house

- No name calling

- Use your manners

- Don't throw food

Further tips on discipline

Your own attitude and behavior will play a vital role in the effectiveness of your discipline. Here are some practical guidelines to take into consideration:

- Focus more on your toddler's good behavior than their mistakes.

- Show and tell your toddler exactly what you want to see and how you want them to behave - otherwise they won't know.

• Focus on specifics, rather than principles. For instance, instead of telling your child to tidy the floor, ask him to pick up his toys.

• Don't bribe by offering a reward if your toddler does something. Keep rewards for good behavior that you didn't have to ask for.

• Practice regular acknowledgement of behaviors that you want.

• Give your toddler unannounced rewards for doing the 'right' thing.

• Begin to give toddlers chores sooner rather than later and encourage them by letting them know how much it has helped you.

• When teaching manners such as 'please' and 'thank you', ignore requests if your toddler doesn't ask correctly. However, don't ignore your child. For example you might refuse to let go of an item you are handing to him until you hear the word 'please'.

• Do your best to be aware of a looming problem so that you can address it before it escalates.

• If you want your child to stop doing something, give him a verbal warning telling him exactly what you want him to do. For example, "If you hit Jack, that will hurt him. Ask him for the toy instead." Make a point of looking into your toddler's eyes and use a gentle yet firm tone of voice.

• When you disapprove of a behavior, it's hurtful to label your toddler as wrong or bad. Let him know that it is his **behavior** that you don't like, not him.

• Telling your child that he's naughty, silly or careless etc. can lead to poor self image and possibly a self fulfilling prophesy.

• Encourage a whingeing toddler to speak in a normal voice "When you speak properly, I'll listen".

• If your toddler refuses to comply with something, let him know the consequences and then keep repeating the option to either cooperate or accept the outcome.

• When having your say mix it with some reassurance to show that it is your child's behavior that you don't like, not him. For instance, you might give a hug or sit him on your lap as you explain what you want or don't want.

• You can often turn a difficult situation around with some fun and giggles. Tickling, silly faces and whispering are some great pressure valve techniques.

• Address bad behavior at the time - don't let your anger escalate. However, if you are so exasperated that you can't speak respectfully, take some of your own 'time out' until you can.

• If your toddler hurts a sibling by biting, for example, respond by initially ignoring the biter and immediately give attention to the bitee. You could then show the biter how he hurt by letting him see the mark on the other one's skin.

• When your toddler has done something to hurt someone, insist that he say "sorry". He will learn a valuable lesson of responsibility and an apology is likely to diffuse a difficult situation.

• As a parent, it is also good for you to say sorry when appropriate. It shows kids that everyone makes mistakes and sets an example of taking responsibility by making amends.

• Be consistent – stay with your rules.

6 HANDLING MISBEHAVIOR

Toddlers have so much to learn. They want to test their boundaries and assert their independence, yet they still fear abandonment. As they grow through this huge learning phase, it's not surprising that children get frustrated and may feel out of control.

Toddlers don't misbehave just because they are little brats or want to annoy you. Before you make a negative judgment, ask yourself why your toddler is being so annoying. Many, if not most behavior problems result from a lack of quality attention.

There is probably an underlying need not being fulfilled and YOU may have to fix the problem. Your toddler may be out of her routine, tired, hungry, over stimulated or physically uncomfortable. She may be feeling jealous and unimportant. Do your best to listen up and respond rather than reacting impulsively.

Early signs of illness are also easy to miss so it's important to be on the alert, because she won't necessarily know how to tell you. For instance, look out for signs such as completely refusing to eat or unusually irritable behavior.

Oftentimes toddlers under two don't even know that their behavior is unacceptable in your eyes. You may be expecting too much from them when they simply don't understand. They may need to be told and repeatedly shown the "right" way to behave.

When toddlers will be toddlers, we have several options open to us. Shouting, showing disgust or punishing your toddler will only make things worse. She will feel misunderstood or even angry and is less likely to trust you.

It is dangerous for a toddler not to trust you. Toddlers need to know that you understand and care. Listening is one of the greatest gifts you can offer anyone. You want your child to grow up feeling that it is safe to confide in you.

Strategies for handling misbehavior

1. Diversion

There are mixed opinions about the use of diversion tactics in this day and age, but it is a tried and proven technique, used for centuries. If you are alert and notice signs of bad behavior looming, seize the moment and divert your toddler's attention away from whatever she was about to do.

However don't expect your child to suddenly and completely forget what she wanted. Divert her attention to something **similar** that is acceptable. You may need to change her environment; move rooms or go outside. Maybe move her play area closer to you.

• Children love water, so think about appropriate ways for them to play with it. They love to chase and pop bubbles. A stash of balloons will never go astray. Even try a fly swat!

• A little stepping stool could be a really handy device to own so that your toddler can see the world from 8" higher.

2. *Pretending to Ignore*

If you pay attention to a behavior - good or bad, you will reinforce that behavior. Sometimes it's best to just turn a blind eye to annoying behavior. As long as no one else is being hurt, your toddler could well stop it because that tactic didn't get your attention. Remember, her attention span is short at this age so she's likely to move on to something else.

3. *'Time out'*

'Time out' is more appropriate once a child turns two. Earlier than that, toddlers just don't get the link between cause and effect. It is important to do 'time out' immediately the problem behavior occurs, otherwise your child will not understand the connection between their action and its consequence.

As a general rule, 'time out' should last for one minute for every year of their age.

'Time out' works for any behavior that you want your toddler to change. Instigate 'time out' to diffuse a situation before it gets completely out of hand. You may give her a count down: "5...4...3...2...", as a warning that this is what you are going to do and then tell her why you are doing it.

Get down to her level and look her in the eye. Use clear words, short sentences and speak with a gentle but firm voice. Remember touch.

'Time out' gives both you and your toddler some breathing space. It is meant to be a cooling off period for both parties - not a punishment.

You may have a chair or stool in a suitable place with no toys or noise around to distract her. Some people use a bathroom, some a bedroom. If it is your toddler's bedroom, don't be concerned that she will link 'time out' with her sleeping place, because 'time out' is literally for such a short time.

Be gently firm. Close, but don't lock the door and leave the scene quickly. Don't wait just outside the room!

When using 'time out' to stop a screaming toddler, give her as much time as she needs to settle down. She may take longer than the two or three minutes.

'Time out' can also be used to get your toddler to do something that she is not cooperating with - such as picking up toys or getting dressed.

4. Withdrawal of privileges

There may be times when none of the above strategies work and you may just have to withdraw some privileges. Once again, this must be done as soon as the behavior occurs.

Dealing with tantrums

There is a lot of material available on ways to deal with toddlers' temper tantrums, but here I will discuss a specific exercise termed the 'Firm Holding Technique' (see endnotes).

'Firm holding' has been proven to be extremely effective as long as you stick with the whole process until your child calms down. The younger your child is when you first use this technique, the faster it will work, both in the long and short term.

Sometimes when children turn on a tantrum, the strength of their feelings scares them. They are feeling out of control, so you are helping them cope with their fears by giving them an "in control" experience.

Firstly, sit down and hold your child with her back to your chest wrapping your arms around her in a gentle and loving way, but firmly enough that you are actually containing her. You hold her legs in between yours so that she can't kick out.

She will fight you and the process could well escalate, so continue to whisper calm messages in her ear. She may well go through a whole cycle of emotions - and might sob very deeply. It is vitally important to keep holding her and continue talking in a clear and soft but firm way until she has calmed down.

This exercise is not easy and it could take quite a while for your child to calm down. However, make sure to see it through so that your toddler ends up having an "in control" experience that restores her to a more peaceful place.

Don't set your child up for failure

For times when you want to go out shopping, for a meal or to the doctor for example, do your best to be prepared. Arm yourself with some toys, snacks and maybe a buggy, because it is too much to expect your little one to behave if she is bored or has excess energy.

Take your own 'time out'

Sometimes it's a good tactic for you to be the one to take 'time out'. This could give a clear indication to your toddler that you are human too and tiring of her behavior. Leave the room for just a minute or three (depending, of course).

Do some deep breathing, count to ten, walk away - whatever works for you. If you take the time for yourself to regain your composure and put things in perspective, you are practicing emotional intelligence and are more likely to remain calm.

CONCLUSION

Hopefully you are now armed with more knowledge about where your toddler is coming from and the motivation to put the important strategies we've discussed into action.

You may not always make the right choices, but if you treat your toddler with the respect he deserves, he will in turn respect you. Your toddler's self-esteem will grow along with your own.

Through these few years, particularly while toddlers are developing at such a fast rate, they need an encouraging, secure and happy environment.

Remember that toddlers crave attention and they will feel valued and happy if you give them time, encouragement and respect.

The communication skills discussed here are especially powerful. Remember to reflect back what you hear so that your toddler feels understood. Children whose feelings are lovingly acknowledged when they are toddlers will grow up with emotional intelligence.

All children need unconditional love - whatever their nature - so it is vital to separate your toddler from his behavior, which can be very trying at times.

The role of discipline is to teach your child about right and wrong so he knows where he stands and learns to take responsibility for his behavior.

When your toddler misbehaves, ask yourself "Why?" You might be able to fix the problem rather than blaming or shaming. Your strategies are more likely to be successful in the long run if you maintain a respectful attitude.

Toddlers will be toddlers. If you work on responding with respect rather than reacting out of anger or frustration, you are more likely to raise a happy, cooperative and emotionally stable child.

Prologue

I trust that you have gained some new insights by reading this book and that it has given you some good food for thought.

The aim was to impart valuable information in a concise and simple read.

If you enjoyed the book, I would really appreciate you leaving a review.

Go to:
http://www.amazon.com/exec/obidos/tg/browse/-/283155 and type in "Toddler Parenting"

Other Recommended Reading:

The Happiest Toddler on the Block

Harvey Karp, M.D.

Love & Logic for Early Childhood

Jim Fay & Charles Fay

Reference:

Firm Holding Technique:

http://www.childbrain.com/pddq11.shtml

.

Made in the USA
Lexington, KY
08 August 2014